Muses of a Successful Businessman

TRAVELING
THE ROAD
THROUGH
 LIFE

*DISCOVERING
THOUGHT
PROVOKING
IDEAS AS
THEY RELATE
TO HUMAN
BEHAVIOR*

*PENNING
THEM SO
OTHERS MAY
ENJOY*

NICHOLAS R DE STEFANO

Muses of a Successful Businessman

Dedication

To Mankind for the many enrichments in my life that I discovered and cherish as I traveled throughout the world.

Contents:

Other books I have written:
- Who Sleeps in Your Skin?
- The Survivor Power Tool Kit/Motivational Power Tools Workshop
- Tools for Success—Understanding the power of the Motivational Power Tools Workshop

Coauthor: How Did You Do That? Became a number one Amazon best seller

Testimonial

Nick De Stefano has been a friend and mentor to me for many years.

Nick is passionate about his desire to share his knowledge and experience about business that he has amassed over a lifetime of the practical application of the principles.

He is dogged in his efforts to teach good business principles so that others might avoid the pitfalls that await anyone who sets out to start a business without the knowledge that they need to succeed.

His written word and videos are stepping stones designed to make it easier to get where you are going and keep your feet dry on the journey.

I wish him well in his noble mission to help others!

Jim Webb

the
webb
w●rks

About the author

Nick is an Entrepreneur, since circa age ten, who recently sold his international jewelry business which he thrived in for over twenty-seven years.

During those twenty-seven years, Nick discovered life enriching particles from other cultures throughout the world as being the same. People of various cultures share in emotional make-up and behavior.

It is that behavior and the reaction to stimuli which has interested Nick for so long. And, he has discovered each of has a uniqueness which sets us apart from the rest.

Moreover, our uniqueness is influenced by subliminal messaging that we are unaware. It is that influence upon our behavior that has interested Nick for so long.

Nick's interest in human behavior and its reaction to stimuli is purely from a natural human behavioral understanding, and not a learned or taught perspective.

Thoughts to Ponder

1. *Don't ever loose who you are!*

   You'll never find yourself again!

   ___

2. *One must remain whole in order to share themselves with another.*

   ___

3. *If you give your heart to someone, what is left of you?*

Who Sleeps in Your Skin?

Have you ever considered that perhaps you are not yourself? You are not whom you think you are?

By this I mean, have you ever considered all the messages you've received while you were growing up that you simply couldn't understand? Subliminal messages that you could not realize? How about all the messages you've received from your parents, teachers, athletic coaches, your preacher or Priest, conscious and un-conscious or, subliminal messages that have negatively or, positively impacted your behavior?

Subliminal messages continue today because you are unaware of them nor do you know how to turn them off or reject them. You continue to receive new messages that reinforce those messages from long ago that plague your consciousness today.

You behave in a certain manner and struggle to know why! Conflicts abound as you struggle to understand your own behavior and, *confusion sets in.*

Consider, all the people in your life who have given you demands to perform in a certain way or, to behave in a certain manner. These behaviors are in contrast to what you would like for yourself. Perhaps you're not aware of the conflicts that have risen within you because these interferences that have been placed upon you by others, all below your conscious level.

Or, you may not have considered any of this at all.

And, you continue in life struggling to understand the many conflicts that rise each day and you pretend to know the reasons why but, these conflicts continue because you do not have the true answers to these conflicts. You continue to be confused but not aware enough to investigate as to the reason why you are confused and maybe suffering.

I would like you to give consideration to the fact that you have simply accepted as fact or true the messages given to you over time. You weren't old enough in thought to challenge these messages or, more likely, you were not aware of these messages or the effect they have had on your behavior.

Is this what is referred to as faith, the blind acceptance of a doctrine or ideal not fully understood?

You've been going along in life feeling a bit distressed but have given no thought as to why. Or, perhaps you have given a *false answer to a conflict* because you simply do not have the true reason for the conflict. You struggle to find an answer to your conflict but, because you have accepted these messages as true, you have no basis for challenging the reason for your conflicts.

A time must come for you to challenge what you have accepted as true!

Remove the confusion in your life so that you may see a clear future for yourself on the horizon.

When that time comes for you, you will give thought to those subliminal messages and challenge their truthfulness for you, today.

When you challenge those messages, using the standards for yourself today, the meaning of those messages will have a different effect for you. You will decide which messages to discard and which to keep.

When you decide to change your behavior and, change your thinking processes, only then will you allow yourself to look at your future with an increased desire to ***empower yourself with positive self-actualization.*** You will then experience the freedom from the constraints of those subliminal messages and move forward in your life, positively and courageously.

You must summon the courage from within you to challenge these messages, see them in today's light, decide what to keep and what not to keep. You will free yourself to be the person you wish to be and make the decisions for you consciously and positively then, you will have empowered yourself with the power and courage to be whom you want to be!

Starting a Business

Many people decide to venture into their own business with little or no knowledge of what it takes to run a business. These brave souls generally are proficient at a particular task or, one simply chooses to be an entrepreneur. Little thought and or preparation is given to the business function itself.

Perhaps the excitement of being an Entrepreneur clouds our eyes to the reality; we ought to know a bit about running a business before starting one.

Or, fueled by the need for independence, they no longer will be required to answer to anyone other than themselves. They may now make their own decisions that will charter the course of their business, changing their lives forever. They alone will make the choices that will create an identity for their new business. They are embarking on a new venture and freedoms not yet experienced, which require different skills than were needed before to maintain this new freedom.

Does this new entrepreneur know the challenges that lie ahead? Do they foresee the challenges, the hidden forces waiting in the darkness of their future that will challenge them to their limits? Likely, they do not. Starting with a Business plan of action coupled with a Marketing plan of action, these instruments if properly prepared, will guide the new entrepreneur successfully into the future.

The most important question to ask is "Why Am I in Business?" Most people will answer "To make money".

If this is the reason you are going into business

"To make money", YOU WILL FAIL!

If you do not have a clear understanding that a business exists to serve its customers, you will fail!

If you do not completely understand that you must provide a useful service or product to mankind, you will fail!

And, I urge you to completely understand the concept of Perceived Value! It is that value that a customer or client will put on your goods or services. You must be cognizant of, and on top of, exactly what that perception is relative to your goods or services, in order for you to be successful.

Your business plan, if properly utilized, will set the course and tone for your business. Your mission statement and purpose will explain WHY you are in business and what you will do to support that mission. Your objectives will be clearly set and a pathway chosen to reach your objectives. Your Marketing plan of action is the fuel needed to drive your business to success.

Within the marketing plan, you will outline the actions needed to obtain the revenue to run your business, the inventory replacement funds, the money necessary to pay all bills as due and, the money needed for salaries. Essentially, where and how will you sell and distribute your products or services that will generate the revenue needed to operate your business. Ponder if you will: it is not good enough to be great at making widgets you must also become proficient at operating the business that is necessary for you to make the widgets. Without the successful operation of the business, your widget making will come to an abrupt end!
Where to start?

You must first decide why you want to be in business.

What service or product are you providing to a customer base that they will need and want and, be willing to buy?

How will you distribute this product or service to the customers? What price will you charge for this product or service and what are the operating expenses?

Will your profit be sufficient for you to effectively operate your business? What will it take to do what you want to do?

Charter a direction for your business.

Where do you want your business to be in one year, five years, and ten years? Have you planned to be successful by preparing a valid business plan of action and a marketing plan of action?

A qualified business consultant or attorney may help with the business plan however; you must also work with a good Marketer to compile the marketing plan of action.

Sharing Knowledge

Why is sharing knowledge relevant and important?

Thinking about industrial or commercial perpetuity or the business of sustaining education…will they survive without transferred knowledge from parting workers to seemingly younger workers or, students whose minds have yet to develop?

Parting workers, usually older workers, have spent decades in studying and analyzing concepts and procedures to facilitate production or movement within an organization that will be lost once they part with the company they presently serve.

Some have referred to this as Brain Drain, the absence of knowledge in the workforce once this exiting process is complete.

Often the parting worker is left with the unproductive activity of his knowledge, *left to wither as if on a dying vine.*

Elder workers are seen by the younger workforce as incapable of or lack the energy or knowledge, to be relevant today.

The irrelevance of knowledge taken from the workplace, lies within the ignorance and minds of the younger worker.

Perhaps through ignorance, disconnection, ego or, some other adjective that describes the arrogance of disallowing shared knowledge. Intimidation comes to mind but, do younger workers lack the knowledge to understand themselves?

I understand the "Can Do" attitude that lies within the ego of the younger worker but, *I also understand the lack of understanding in what the younger worker does not know.*

It seems so simple from afar, to look back and see this all acting out in our understanding of the matter.

Unfair to the elderly, you say? Unfair to the consumer, you say? Unfair to the economy, you say?

I say, Unfair to Mankind!

So much has transpired in creating the environment in which we live today.

Hasn't it been the result of the older workers' contribution to mankind that has created this *opportunity* for us today?

That opportunity is whatever you wish it to be!

That is the contribution of the retiring worker. The *opportunity* that we *glean* today from the activities of others that have gone before us, was created by a mind that will no longer be available to us in perpetuity--lost forever.

Think about Albert Einstein and the many contributions to mankind he left behind for us to traverse to this point in time. Wouldn't we be much more educated if his mind was still available to us? Of course!

And, in a way, his mind is still with us in that we have recordings of his accomplishments and contributions to mankind.

But, do we have the use of his mind today?

May we get a response from this learned mind for a present-day equation needing to be solved? Of course, not.

With this short essay about knowledge lost, we can see the value to mankind in retaining the minds of departing workers in that they will share their knowledge with us to *facilitate the next great happening for mankind?*

Capturing the minds of departing workers will create an environment and library of knowledge for mankind that will facilitate growth and development into perpetuity.

A departing mind, withering on a decaying vine, is lost knowledge, forever gone, never again to assist mankind in developing further.

Casting aside the minds that have created your environment, the world in which you participate, is *counter-productive to mankind's perpetuity.*

Marketing

Or the lack of effective Marketing

Marketing is a misunderstood term.

Often misused and mostly misunderstood by those of us who use the term, "Marketing" has been used to describe a process of, or involvement in, sales, advertising (print, video, air) or, customer service, customer support or, telemarketing (people using the telephone to call potential customers with an offer of some kind) internet sales and, sometimes a performance by one in a similar persuasion.

Marketing defined:
According to Merriam Webster's Collegiate Dictionary (Tenth Edition) the word MARKETING: "1. A: the act or process of selling or purchasing in a market b: the process or technique of promoting, selling, and, distributing a product or service 2: an aggregate of functions involved in moving goods from prouder to consumer"

The aggregate functions are described as:

- A. Advertising
- B. Distribution
- C. Promotion
- D. Sales
- E. Customer Service
- F. And, some may argue the inclusion of Research and Development (R & D).

And, one may argue that Marketing is a social function as well. During the process of moving products from production to the consumer, especially today with many multi-level marketing programs, social media and, networking opportunities that we encounter along the way.

When asked "what is your job function" one often answers, "I'm in Marketing". Although this may be a correct response, the answer itself conveys nothing to the audience of what one actually does or in what part of Marketing one may perform or participate nor does this answer make clear or address an area of expertise.

With this answer, it is my opinion that a listener lacks an understanding of the job performance of this individual and is left to question exactly what does this speaker do. I would think that rather than engaging a listener in conversation, this answer may leave only questions in the listener's mind. I think a response like this unintentionally ignores what the person actually does and may be counterproductive in its application, i.e. failing to clearly present to the listener an understanding of one's job performance or area of expertise.

Arguably, do we understand the difference between Marketing and Sales?

The person or firm using the term Marketing instead of the actual job description may somehow feel entitled or empowered by using this term, perhaps for effect rather than accuracy. Or perhaps one may feel elevated to a higher class or standard than that of a *mere* salesperson or one who may be an advertiser!

I question one's validity in choosing the term Marketing to explain their job performance. What does this answer really convey to the listener? Does this answer clearly state what the speaker does within Marketing?

I beg you, what is wrong or politically incorrect with a SALESPERSON saying or referring to the SELLING process as that to which one is engaged? What is wrong or incorrect by telling someone that you are in print or radio Advertising, as an example? Can it be they themselves have a negative connotation to the job that they are engaged?

Or, is it that they have a misconception of selling or the selling process and in some way, may feel empowered by using the term marketing; does it somehow soften or redirect someone's thinking for a more favorable response? Clearly, the answer "I am in marketing" profoundly clouds the response by creating a non-transparent answer to a very simple question!

This brings up a question. What is our understanding or interpretation of the selling or advertising process? Why must we change the name of what we do?

Fear!

Yes, fear! I think we either consciously or unconsciously fear rejection or non-acceptance should we profess our involvement as a sales person or advertiser. We clearly understand that some have a negative perception of salespeople and the function of sales but, this is the profession some of us have chosen. So why is it that we prefer to hide behind a cloud? Why do we not declare ourselves to be a professional salesperson?

Interestingly, I believe that we choose words that we *think* would have a favorable impact upon our intended target when we are seeking a more favorable response to ourselves--seeking approval or acceptance.

I believe we justly receive the misunderstanding of what we do because we fail to correctly and completely inform our target of *what* it is that we actually do. This of course results in confusion with the lack of clarity.

Must this charade persist? Must we continue to wear this false façade impressing no one?

Consider this: A salesperson might offer the following answer to the question, *"what do you do?"* The salesperson may say something like "I provide performance benefits to my clients in their advertising campaign, such as…. (describe the benefits and performance one should expect from this service)".

By describing what one will do to advertise their clients' product or service, frequency and quality of their services and how they differ from their competition, the speaker is demonstrating confidence, not only in himself but also in his knowledge and expertise, and confidence in themselves as a professional salesperson.

This answer does not only demonstrate knowledge of the task at hand it also demonstrates an understanding of their competition including their products and services and, that one has the expertise needed to conquer the competition with favorable results for the customer.

A simple exercise for clarity ought to answer any question one may have as to which choice would be more appropriate, informative and, clear to the intended listener.

The exercise? Simply, ASK THEM! Ask your intended audience what their choice would be. Conduct a little marketing research!

Which would be more beneficial to the listener? Providing them a clear and complete description of your job performance or offering the answer I'M IN MARKETING? Which answer would you prefer?

Ponder if you will the concept that one truly believes in the work they are doing. One believes they are offering benefits and services that will truly enhance the value of life to those who accept them and, they are proficient in what they do.

They are knowledgeable and professional in their careers. They understand their competition and their products. They value and appreciate those around them. They care about performance excellence for their customers. They are positive and creative.

Would this person not want to tell a prospect what they do? Would they not want to inform everyone that they encounter just how they could benefit from using these goods or services? Would this person not want to tell everyone they are a professional salesperson with valuable products that will benefit them and their family?

I am sure one who declares himself/herself a professional and competent salesperson would want to tell everyone exactly and clearly who they are and what they do!

Make yourself feel great again

We are born to be free!

What happens is, we're pressured to conform to what other's think we should be, follow their rules, not the rules of nature.

Our *freedom* depends on how well we *BEHAVE*, that is to follow the orders of our superiors, our handlers and dance to the beat of their drum.

What happened to individuality, free spirit, creativity?
We are not allowed to be free, to show our uniqueness, our strengths or, to express our desires. We are taught to conform, follow the rules. This happens when we reach the age of about three, when our handlers think we are old enough to comply with their demands. We are no longer the free spirits as we were born! We must change our behavior and, conform, they demand from us.
Prior to age three, we are *free* to express ourselves, and ***demonstrate our uniqueness!***
We as children learn to express ourselves, find pleasure playing with a bottle cap, learn to walk, jump, try to talk, all the FUN things to do while celebrating LIFE and our *freedom.*

For nine months, we are trapped in the womb then, we discover freedom only to be trapped again!
Then one day, our world comes crashing down around us because some handler demands that we give up our individuality and conform to their way of thinking, to behave in the manner they perceive for us, follow their rules!

Rebel, we must! Take back our freedom!
It's time to return to our days of yesteryear!

Rise up! Let's bring back the fun in our lives, recreate the atmosphere in which we were free, allow our spirits to roam, demonstrate our individuality and,
allow our uniqueness to be shared with mankind!

Have you watched a kitten develop? When a kitten is born, the mother cat does not restrict the newborn. The kitten is allowed its freedom unless it happens upon danger, at which time mother cat intervenes and returns the kitten to a safe haven.

In time, as the kitten grows, it develops while exploring its world, expressing its uniqueness while sharing with the rest of its family. The kitten grows and shares its knowledge with other cats, to be repeated.

Observing nature, we may take from nature and learn to be more playful and less demanding, not to interfere with our individuality and expression of who we are!

We will learn to be free and feel great!

Leading from within

I think many of us have not realized our true potential for leadership.

Is leadership something we are taught to master or are we born to be a leader?

The failure to recognize our uniqueness may keep us from reaching the top of our leadership potential robbing others of our unique abilities to make a positive difference for mankind.

How many leaders are naturally born? Not many I believe. Some, yes.

Leaders achieve greatness by acquiring many skills along the way and effectively using those skills to be the master of their game. They learn to ignore their insecurities and instead concentrate on their strengths, lead by example and train those below themselves in leadership.

Each and every one of us is created with a unique set of values and abilities. The problem is, we are not encouraged to uncover and use those abilities and values.

We are taught more to follow another and learn from that successful leader more than we are encouraged to be creative and use our natural talents.

I do not mean to imply that learning from others has no value. There is much to gain by studying and emulating successful leaders.

I am suggesting, we learn more about ourselves and by doing so, we will learn to incorporate our uniqueness into our leadership, developing our own style. Perhaps we do this subconsciously but, I think by deliberately inquiring of ourselves, we will have a far greater impact on our performance as a leader of mankind. Concentrating on our uniqueness, we can deliver a far more impacting style that is easily for us to assume because, it is ourselves that we emulate.

From the beginning, I believe we are subliminally impregnated with negative thoughts and ideas about who we are and what we should be. Seldom if ever are we encouraged to discover our natural genius and use that talent to make a difference in our world.

Perhaps our mentors have not understood what it is I am about to discuss with you. And that is the idea of uncovering your core values and beliefs-- those core values that are uniquely yours--the core values that set you apart from all others.

Each and every one of us has within ourselves those core values, when nurtured to fulfillment, will be our gift to mankind.

Knowledge

Do we acquire it? Is it innate?

Or, is it that both are within us?

Or, is it neither?

Often, I have wondered, which is correct—right or wrong?

How do we learn?

Is learning knowledge?

Does possessing knowledge mean that we learn?

Or, is it what we do with what we learn that creates our knowledge?

Does being right mean, you are not wrong?

How do I know if I am right or wrong?
Does time of itself, mean that one learns or acquires knowledge?

What does time have to do with knowledge?
Do we gain knowledge with the passing of time?
One thing is for certain, in time we will pass with whatever knowledge we
have.

Journey, An Invitation

A life changing experience!

Come, join me on my journey through life filled with freedom, creative love, mysterious adventures, exciting world travels.

An exuberant journey filled with success and happiness.
An abundance of riches well beyond your imagination are awaiting you to enjoy.

A gratefulness of life seldom experienced by others-all for you to appreciate and embrace.

Simply join me and experience a well-balanced life that is filled with riches beyond your imagination--a life filled with love and prosperity.

It's been quite a while now since I began my journey in life towards my destiny.

Intuitively at birth, it started with a cry of relief where I was no longer in darkness-escaping from the protective womb--free now to be whomever I choose. My heart felt as if I were a free spirit-I was now able to choose the life that I preferred and desired without restraints. I am now free to navigate towards my destiny with a childlike unencumbered exuberance.

Why not? I was given no instructions while in the womb. Nor had I received a manual or script to guide me on my journey in life.

May I not choose for myself my path to destiny? I am born without restrictions, free from capture to be as I choose to be in life while I may in some way benefit mankind.

My choices in life will guide me towards my destiny; no one else can do that for me. I have the power of choice to experience my current's flow and to explore the various paths of adventure along the way towards my destiny

.

I choose to experience and navigate the curves and challenges in life as they present themselves without prior restrictions.

I am experiencing a shared existence with that of the mighty river.

A river has its origin and is continuously flowing towards its destiny. Dam the river and it will find another path to its destiny. It will not be stopped or deterred but, rather it will always and deliberately flow to its destiny. Nothing will prevent a river from accomplishing its goal of reaching its destiny!

The river is forever inviting! Share with it the pleasures and beauty of its current flow. Navigate its waters--it asks for nothing in return. Experience and enjoy what the river has to offer mankind--one need not give or pledge something in return--the river asks only that you enjoy what it has to offer!

By inviting one to join me on my journey and to navigate the current of my river's flow, together we shall share in the many adventures along the way towards destiny. A life filled with adventures and excitement far beyond our imagination. A life filled with an abundance of prosperity and goodness.

And, experience the excitement of chance encounters as we fill our lives with adventures and opportunities yet encountered. These we shall share if we are free of negative and entrapping principles and ideals of meaningful others. These we shall share if we ask for nothing in return!

For the young, handlers sometimes choose a path of restraint, possessiveness and, control--all of which they claim to be in your best interest! Humph!

Could it be. perhaps the choice of others is a manifestation of their fears or, perhaps their unwillingness to indulge or participate in another's creativity--faulting to apathy--wanting to stay in their safe zone, a perceived safe place for themselves?

How real is that?

It went so terribly wrong

an enhancing victory

I got a call from someone I apparently met at a networking event, asking if I'd be interested in an exchange of services.
He said he was a Harvard Journalist on call, an accomplished writer and self-published author…would I agree to meet with him?

He offered: in exchange for his writing in my blog, I would agree to provide a link back to his website. Didn't sound so terrible. The prospect piqued my curiosity so I agreed to meet with this person and get the details.

In my mind, I thought this meeting could be great for me because I have been struggling with writing my latest book and it would be a good idea to make friends with someone so accomplished.

What crossed my mind was, if this person is so successful, why is he contacting me? I am small potatoes and could hardly offer him a good acknowledgement.

When he approached me, I was immediately struck by his unkemptness; he needed a hair-cut and clean clothes. The shirt he wore looked like it hadn't been washed for a long time with its shirt collar curled at the fold. It looked very dirty to me. Was he as well?

Immediately, I was taken aback thinking, was this person successful?

I believe *success comes from within, not something determined by what others think success is for another.*

But, when one has reached a point of success in their mind, usually it follows that a good appearance would reflect how one thinks of himself. At least, that has been my experience, one always wants to make a good impression.

The next thing I noticed about him was his *insincerity.*

He asked me a question and, without listening for my reply, he bound right into what he was going to do for me, that he would make me successful, *for a price of course.*

WOW, all this from someone I've just met who knows nothing about me or my accomplishments nor did he think that I may consider myself successful.

When I asked why he thought I was not successful, he pointed to a comment I made about not having sold a number of books that I would like to have sold.

His assumption was, I am not successful. His assumptions of me didn't stop there, however.

I felt he was being very unprofessional in his dialog, not ever asking me what I thought of his ideas.

He ranted on about how successful he was, that he has helped so many others and, how I needed his services to make me successful. He finally got around to how he could help me with my new book. He didn't ask about specifics, only that he will make me very successful.

While flipping through the pages of my three books that I brought along to discuss with him, he tells me there is no content in these books, they won't sell. He may be right but, I thought it would be best to at least read through the books first, before making any comment about them.

I am beginning to feel a con coming.

He would make me successful he said, by writing my book collaboratively with me and in conjunction with his marketing.

WOW, I was to be so impressed with this offer that I was to jump at the opportunity to pay him ten-thousand dollars to help me!

All the time this person talked, not once did he make eye contact with me. As he talked, I noticed he not just glanced his gaze past me rather, he looked past me completely.

My experience tells me that if someone will not look you in the eye as they are speaking to you, do not trust them.
Trusting my instincts; I do not trust this person! How could I even think to pay this person ten-thousand dollars to help me write my new book? Was this the con or, was there more to come?

Thinking I am about to get ripped-off, I chose to end this conversation telling him that I didn't trust someone who made such accusations or assertions of one's success and, without taking the time to know more about that other person or his limitations and aspirations.

I left the conversation convinced I had just witnessed a potential con upon myself!

Always trust your instincts!

It's lonely at the top

- Eggs over easy.
  - Eggs over medium.
    - Eggs over hard.
      - Scrambled is better?

Decisions, decisions!

Entrepreneurs constantly face daunting challenges. Hopefully not about breakfast!

There isn't a day that goes by that an entrepreneur isn't faced with making a business decision that may offend some and please others.

A decision usually is made in the company's best interest because it is the survival of the business that will perpetuate the very existence of that business and solidify the jobs for workers.

Of course, consideration must be given to individual team players as well but overall the leader must know what the overall optimal decision must be and one must toughen the skin so to speak for the betterment of the business. And, sometimes that may be an unpopular decision but a fair and just one as well.

Too often an entrepreneur will find himself in a lonely place fending off the wolves that may want to harm his company. He must be steadfast and certain in his decision making and not waver. His workers must see him as a pillar of strength and above human frailties because it is he that they rely upon to run the business smoothly and profitably in order to secure their jobs.

Especially in smaller companies, the entrepreneur is the sole executive with no one else to turn for advice or guidance. This executive must show strength and determination.

As the leader of this company one must not hesitate nor waver in their determination less his subordinates become insecure in their jobs and loose trust in their leader.

The result of confused or threatened employees is low morale and reduced or shoddy production--one to avoid at all cost.

So, when one needs reassurance and support and he is at the top, where does he go to get support?

It can be very lonely at the top but, if one has complete faith, decisiveness and self-assurance, being lonely at the top one can experience a very peaceful existence!

Imagination
If you listen well…

If you listen well, you will experience a new reality based on your perception of the picture I am about to paint for you.

Allow yourself to be drawn away, carried to a place of pleasure where the air is crisp and inviting. A place never witnessed by you but, you will understand immediately and completely. A place filled with Amore waiting for you to visit and enjoy the pleasures it offers, exclusively for you.

I want to take you on a journey to a place far away, where you will experience the delight and total pleasure and, completely of your making.

Navigate to:

- Ancient Rome
- The leaning tower of Pizza
- A place where you will witness the rolling hills of Tuscany
- Experience a ride in the Gondolas on the glistening waters of Venice
- A place where you can smell the pasta sauce cooking over the Hearth with Amore
- A place where the wafer of garlic fills the air, a glass or two of Vino
- A place where Momma is Queen
- A place where the table cloths are red and white, checkered
- A place filled with Amore and Abbondanza

Bon Appetito

Ciao

A Strange dream

I awoke from a strange dream this morning.

In my dream, I could not ascertain who the owner of a business was, that I wanted to contact. For some reason, I struggled to determine between two, who the actual owner was.

I talked with others trying to identify with whom I should talk, as the owner of this business. Not only did I talk with others, I went from place to place in hopes of finding my answer, to no avail.

Therefore, I was unable to effectively communicate with the true owner of this business.

As my grogginess faded from my brain, I felt I was looking for myself!

Thinking that; I have a difficult time describing just who I think I am and how I help people in business. So, I thought about that for a little bit and wondered how it is that I cannot describe myself to myself!

Geeze! If I can't describe myself to myself, how can I effectively describe what I do, or who I am, for others?

I resolve the complexities of business for others.
So, I sat down to write my thoughts to try and identify and communicate my complexity to myself, so that others will grasp how it is that I may assist them in their business.

I have maintained that I am a management and marketing expert for entrepreneurs; a business consultant and coach.

So, What! This understanding has not developed my business. I continue to search for the owner…

I know I inspire others to act. I help others see things in a different light. I encourage others to not despair, hope is here.

I wrote Who Sleeps In your Skin? with the hope of inspiring others to greatness.

I wrote the Survivor Power Tool Kit, a motivational work to encourage participation in the Motivational Power Tools Workshop where they could learn to be more logical in their thinking when confronted with a situation or a problem needing to be solved.

Isn't that who I think I am? A person who thinks logically?
But, it seems others are not accepting how I may help them, if indeed they need my help, because I am not able to simply state Who or How I can help someone; do they in fact need my help?

Yes, most people need my help in sorting out the complexities they are faced with on a daily bases. That being said, how do I get this message to them in the hope that they will hire me for that purpose?

I said, I am a management and marketing expert for entrepreneurs. While that is true, it isn't very exciting; it doesn't get one to react and hire me; to do what?

I am stumbling, going from one place to another, not trying to find myself but rather, to find the words to express myself, simply and effectively where one would want to act in hiring me.

Is simply stating that I help to inspire others good enough for one to act? I don't think so. Does telling others that I motivate and inspire one, good enough? I don't think that statement is good enough either.

I search and search within to come up with the right words to simply describe how I may help another.
I wrote, Tools for Success with the idea of walking one through a scenario where a business man, who is struggling to keep his business afloat, finds usage in the tools from the Motivational Power Tools Workshop to save himself and his business from collapse.

In my dream, I am looking for the owner of a business and finding confusion in determining the rightful owner so that I may continue with communicating whatever it is that I wanted to talk about, to the rightful owner of that business.
It seems to me that I am the rightful owner of that business that I am searching for and, now that I have discovered the rightful owner, I am failing to communicate!

I am struggling to come up with the right words to describe how I may help an entrepreneur to help them run their business.

In my heart, I know. Getting that knowledge to someone is the difficulty. I have been unable to describe to myself, just who I am, I am so complex.

I am my best fan! But, I fail in making my case as to how I will help others.

Because I personally have navigated through some of the treacherousness of being, I know how I can help others navigate through their circumstances, successfully.
Knowing something and, having someone receive the positive message is where my discomfort and failure lie.

I have yet to discover the words to describe my capabilities that will help others. If I cannot solve a problem for them, why do they need me? I must identify a need in them that I can resolve.

Everyone has a problem to be solved. Using the right words to uncover a hidden problem is my block.
They will not hire me if I cannot demonstrate that I will solve their pain— put out their fire.

Have you ever asked?

- Where has the time gone?
- How do I find time to do all the things in life that I want to do?
- How will I find more time to spend with my family, my friends, my hobbies?
- Why do I find it difficult to delegate activities to others?
- How can I increase my productivity?
- What are my High Payoff Activities?
- Where is my life headed?
- Where is my business headed--is it going in the right direction?
- As a business person, am I choosing the best marketing strategy for my business?

At times, we may want to relax our management skills in favor of what is easy for us to do.

When we forget to use effective communication, we risk losing the spirit of productivity.

Without effective communication, how do we empower our teams?

And, in the end, if we fail to realize how much our personal life is entangled with our business we fail to realize how important it is to have balance in our world.

Our business is not our life--our business is a PART of our life.

Each day we have many demands of our time both personal and professional. Time is what we have to manage. We cannot insert hours into our day and we cannot control the universe.

However, we can control the *use* of our time. What we do with the minutes and hours of each day should be carefully orchestrated to deliver a better quality of life and balance within our family and profession.

How do we do that?

The answers to these questions lie within you.

You have the solution to your own demise or survival. You have the final answers to control yourself, your business and, your prosperity.

What and how you do it will enhance your life and increase your productivity.

Driving me self-crazy

Okay, so you are a successful entrepreneur with many years' experience doing what it is that you do. You started a business and you have made a lot of money-but are you successful? There is a storm ahead as you drive off, wondering.

You are driving along reflecting on what a great job you have done directing your business-or, have you done a great job?

After all you have something that a lot of people want and are willing to pay for-so, are you really that important in your own business, you muse.

Of course, your ego is larger than life so you really can't ask for assistance should you deem something needing change--or can you? You are the one who has brought your company this far so, why would you ask for assistance from anyone?

Except perhaps, you think, if I am to move this company forward, how will I do that? Admittedly, I am limited in my training in running a business but, could my ego allow me to ask for assistance?

And, where would I find this assistance; of course if I needed it!

That storm is approaching faster and faster, closer and closer. This doesn't look like an ordinary storm you muse; it looks like it is going to be a huge storm-the wind is picking up, fast!

Suddenly, it is getting very dark outside and all of a sudden you see a stranger on the side of the road hitch-hiking. You give thought to giving him a ride but you remind yourself to be cautious in times like this. Is this a safe thing to do? What harm might come to you?

The storm is approaching faster now and you have little time to decide-will you help this person or allow him to drown in the ensuing and inevitable Monsoon?

In the back seat of your car sits this stranger whom you have just rescued and, you are feeling very good about that. Before long you both start to chatter and become friendly sharing personal thoughts with each other. In the past you would have given in to caution, why not today?

Before long you are talking about your desires to move your business forward; with this stranger you may say whatever you want and feel safe, right? Why you will never see this stranger again once you drop him off. And, you begin to feel relief from the pressures of running your business and suddenly you give thought to how good that feels!
You are feeling the tension in your shoulders disappear;
you're breathing slowing to a normal pace; your heart rate slowing to a normal beat.

You are amazed at how good you now feel just by sharing thoughts that have claimed tension and disturbance within you for so long. And, you notice how clearly you begin to think and how less protective of yourself you are feeling.

You begin to tell this stranger of your weaknesses in moving your business forward but of course, that is only a passing thought. What would he think of you if you shared your feelings of insecurity?

A slip of the tongue in your conversation reveals to the stranger in the back seat just how worried you are about your inability to move your business forward and perhaps failure, if you do not.

All of a sudden you wake up! You had fallen asleep at your desk heavy in thought and burdened with feelings of unwanted pressures of worry that had befallen you.

You are awakened by a knock on your door. A stranger has come in from the storm outside and may he share a few minutes with you till the storm passes?

Lightning is striking all around your building, the rain being driven by powerful winds. You cannot say no to this stranger and send him out in that!
You allow the stranger to sit with you awhile and before long you begin to talk. Cautiously at first as in your dream. And, as in your dream, you begin to share your thoughts with a stranger.

The stranger listens carefully and then says, I am sent here by a hitch hiker you recently…

Competition

Why do you think you have competition?

Whether you are a business owner, a representative of a business or, a worker in a corporate venue, chances are you think you have competition.

You're likely to think I'm crazy when I tell you that the competition you think you have is between your ears. That's right! The competition you think you have is just that, a thought, an idea planted there by someone or something, yourself for that matter; a process or a duplication from what other's may have said and, to conform, you agree.

I am here to tell you that you absolutely have no competition in whatever it is that you do. As a business owner, corporate colleague or, a representative of a business, you have no competition!

Or, as a US Olympic athlete:

Did Matthew Centrowitz have competition in the Men's 1500?

Did Michael Phelps have competition in the water?

Did Simone Biles have competition in gymnastics?

As you ponder: how can that be, no competition? You go on to say, there are so many competitors in my field, that it's impossible not to have competition.

Really?

Well, the answer lies within you! The answer to competition lies within your belief system.

You think it quite normal to have competition! But, if I tell you it's normal NOT to have competition, what would you say to me? Be nice!

You have been raised to believe competition rules the world.

It's because of competition that our economy thrives; isn't that what you believe? Isn't that what you've been told? Of course it is. I believed that for quite some time as well, until that day!

It was that day that I faced a menace, a danger that I needed to overcome in order to survive. I felt as if I had no choice but to survive but how, in the face of all this competition?
I found the answer. The answer is within me.

It is that answer I am going to share with you.

But first, let me tell you a short story.

I had been fired from fourteen jobs in less than twelve years. Yes, fourteen jobs!

I was going through a divorce, not much money in my pocket and a much deflated ego. I had just been told my present job was being terminated because the distributor of major appliances I was working for was going out-of-business.

And, the day before this happened, I bought a new car, with car payments.

WOW! What do I do now?

I had always wanted to be in business for myself—actually, I was in business for myself when I was a shoe-shine boy about twelve years of age. But, this was different. This was real! But, how do I just go into business?

I have a degree in business and a major in management with a minor in economics. Is that enough to go into business as an adult? What did I know about business? At age twelve, it didn't matter—I had moxie!

As an adult, was moxie enough to go into business? I didn't know but, I do have courage and courage is what I needed!
With very little money I did the easiest thing there was for me to do and that was buy and sell costume jewelry to retail stores. I continued to buy and sell until I got very good at it—buy low and sell as high as I could. This went on for a few years until I reached the doors of the big time. When I had to go head-to-head with the big boys I realized there was no way for me to compete with them.

I reached the summit of my career only to be confronted with a decision that would change my career and my philosophy regarding competition, forever.

Courage was no longer enough! I needed to do something, and quickly! There was no way for me to retreat! I had a taste of entrepreneurship and I loved that taste! I wasn't going back!

What to do? How could I stay in business after coming this far and meeting the big boys? Failure appeared certain but, I couldn't allow that to happen.

And, it did not happen!

I continued to grow and operate my business until I sold my business after twenty-seven years and never had a competitor. I had over seven-hundred customers when I sold my business. Yes, my customers bought from the big boys too.

What I sold is what I will share with you, now.

I realized there was no way I could possibly compete with these big boys especially, on their terms. I could not compete with these million-dollar companies because I had no money to compete with them.

I operated my business with Vendor Capitalization.
It took a little thinking for me to realize that first, I was not one of them, the big boys.

I was a little business in a big world but, there was room for me if I didn't try to be competitive but, just be me! I realized that what I had to offer the big boys didn't have and, that was me!

No, this is not about inflated ego! This is about reality! I could only do what I could do and, that was not try and compete with the big boys.

I studied the big boys and learned from them. I decided to offer our customers something the big boys didn't have but, the customers wanted.

My realization was that I needed to be me and provide to my customers what they wanted in the way that I could provide.

That concept, while so simple, became so big. It worked extremely well, so much so, that my philosophy about competition has evolved to what I am sharing with you, now.

Stop trying to compete! Be yourself!

Know who you are, understand your uniqueness, offer what you are capable of offering. Be at the top of your game. There is no other in this world like you. There may be others similar as you but, they are not you nor do they have your uniqueness!

No one can offer this universe what you have to share with mankind!

Simply and confidently, tell the world how you will benefit mankind and help them prosper from your creation! Know yourself-your uniqueness-that will benefit mankind in a way no other can!

Simply present your uniqueness as a benefit for mankind to prosper.

You will come to understand:

YOU HAVE NO COMPETITION BUT YOURSELF!

Branding

Branding is considered the visual, sound, slogan, logo, trademark or other advertisements, when used by the Brand to identify the Brand, that will result in a thought process with the consumer to lead back to that which the Brand does and is.

Branding a product, company or, an idea is not a mere slogan, saying, product mark or design that captures the essence and style of the BRAND; what the Brand stands for, what a recipient will receive from the brand and at the same time provides a visual, sound and sight of what is branded that one will receive from the brand.

BRANDING must have VALUE!

Essentially, when one sees a logo hears a sound or sees the capture of art as representation of the BRAND, that is considered BRANDING!

Branding is not one thing to describe an area, place, a company or a thing. Branding is a sequence of and a compilation of all that will encompass what is branded.

Family Business

Growing a business is not unlike developing a family.
As the head of a family business, your objective for the business may have failed to reach the rest of the family.

Your partners in this family business have their own idea as to where they see this family business going but, they in turn have failed to tell their story to the rest of the family.

The growing family members, being the unique individuals as they are, have expectations of their own as to where their personal growth should be headed but have failed to discuss this with the rest of the family as well.

WOW! Where is this family headed?

It doesn't take a mathematician or rocket scientist to see that this family is headed for failure.

Yet, isn't this what we see in US businesses today?
Why is this scenario played out in businesses over and over again?

Clearly, the lack of communications!

If communications are not driven from the top down, how will the supporting members of the team know what is expected of them? If leadership feels they have no guidance, what is to be expected of them? Poor communications results in poor production and poor quality!

Clearly communicating with each other eliminates confusion and, in some cases hostility.

Is Your Business Running You?
Or, are You Running Your Business?

Have you ever asked:

- Where has the time gone today?
- How do I find time to do all the things in life that I want to do?
- How will I find more time to spend with my family, my friends, my hobbies?
- Why do I find it difficult to delegate activities to others?
- How can I increase my production, my sales?
- What are my High Payoff Activates?
- Where is my business headed--is it going in the right direction?
- Marketing? Am I choosing the best marketing strategy for my business?

Often, business is started with fresh ideas lots of enthusiasm and, a great deal of hard work. As time goes by and the business builds we may fail to realize the value of time management, the value of delegation and, the value in following a well-documented business and marketing plan.
At times, we may want to relax our management skills in favor of what is easy.

When we forget the value of effective communication we lose our spirit and also lose our productivity and we no longer (or never did) empower our team members and in the end, we failed to execute the value of prioritizing!
Often, we fail to realize how much our personal life is entangled with our business life and if we do understand, we fail to realize how important it is

to have balance in our world. Our business is not our life-our business is a PART of our life.

Your business ought not define you.

You ought to define your business.

Each day we have many demands on our time both personal and professional. Time is what we have to manage. We cannot insert hours into our day and we cannot control the universe.

However, we can control the *use* of our time. What we do with the minutes and hours of each day should be carefully orchestrated to deliver a better quality of life and balance within our family and profession.

How do we do that? The answers to these questions lie within you. You have the solution to your own demise or survival. You have the final answers and control to grow your business to prosperity.

With so many books on time management solutions--how many can you read? Now there is an outstanding program offered to inspire you to do great things with the time you have. What and how you do it will enhance your life and increase your productivity.

As a business mentor, I have several programs that are extremely effective in helping one to refocus and add value to their lives.
A program can be a very effective tool for one to learn the values that lie within themselves and how to use them.
You will learn to refocus on the important things and learn to delegate those tasks that have less value. You will learn to use your time more

effectively and discover the EXTRA time within the day to do those tasks that are very important and profitable to you.

You will learn to run your business and not have your life run *by* your business.

Learning to effectively handle interruptions. Discover the power of empowering your team.

Learn to prioritize your actions for optimal results.

An Effective Sales Presentation

Ponder if you will the concept that you truly believe in the work you do. You believe you offer benefits and services that will enhance the value of those who accept them.

- You are proficient in what you do.
- You are knowledgeable and professional in your career.
- You understand your competition and their products.
- You value and appreciate those around you.
- You care about performance excellence for your customers.
- You are positive and creative.

Undoubtedly, you want to tell everyone you meet just how they could benefit from using your goods or services. And, you want to demonstrate to everyone that you are a professional salesperson with valuable products that will benefit them and their family.

I am sure one who declares himself/herself a professional and competent salesperson would want to demonstrate to everyone exactly and clearly who they are and what they do! You want to help others. Courageously, you move forward giving your message to all that will listen.

But, and there is a "but"; it is not about you, it is ALL about them!

No matter how well you present yourself, product or service, you may not be heard. Studies have shown that you have twenty seconds to get someone's attention. If they do not see in their mind's eye the picture you are creating, they will mentally turn you off--there is nothing in your presentation for them! No matter how good your services are unknowingly, you have failed to address the listeners' issues and desires.

Example: I recently asked a client what his main recruiting problem was in his business. His answer was "Finding qualified candidates". After further discussion, I discovered that he was telling candidates how great his business was and, that he had great products to sell. He assumed all candidates were interested in his success but he failed to get their attention; they tuned him out.

They were waiting for "What's in this for me?"

He did not ask, they did not tell! He never addressed the candidates' concerns or motivations.

Until you discover the wants and needs of your audience they will never hear your message. Your message must address their needs and desires. Their unanswered question: what do I get from this? Will they experience your genuine concern for them if you are not addressing their needs?

Address their issues and they will listen and hear what you have to say and respond favorably.

Coming to this earth

We, at birth, although created in kind are uniquely special and very different from each other.

Although we appear to be the same--humans--we have very different and distinct values, gifts to share and, qualities that no other has to share with mankind.

I think very few of us come to realize how special and different we are. Most of us go throughout life trying to find out just who they are. And, trying to *fit into* society--to conform.

Why?

It could very well be because of the children who raised us! Children? Yes, our parents, aunts, uncles, teachers, neighbors; yes of course. Children see these mentors as adults, all knowing and wise? Anyone older than the child would be considered a person in charge, an adult whose word at times, is magic or even Gospel.

Isn't it our responsibility to create the path of awareness for our young? I think it's time for us to facilitate awareness training in our young to help them understand the uniqueness that is theirs alone? Not better or worse than anyone else just simply, unique.

Furthermore, we can show our appreciation for the uniqueness in others as well. I think we need to demonstrate our understanding of the uniqueness in children by allowing them flexibility in their behavior to foster creativity and confidence in themselves.

Instead, what we do is foster compatibility by requiring children to conform to certain behavioral styles, often different styles than their own natural style.

Moreover, I think this leads to much confusion in a child as in development especially, when a child cannot differentiate behavioral styles.

It's time for us to allow the young to be who they naturally are rather than for us to try and have them fit into a mold in our society. They need to be creative and always moving forward to a better future for themselves--not a future someone else thinks a child should have.

Nurture a child to be as he ought to be naturally, not as we think they ought to be.

A Family Divided

A house that falls

Like any structure, a house is the sum of its parts, some parts weaker than others, the weaker only strengthened by the stronger.

Thus, it is with family--the core from which we descend, some stronger than others, others weaker but, supported by the stronger--w*e survive!*

The family unit is primeval to all--a unit created by the sum of its parts that make up the core of the unit of which is family. Without the core, there can be no family unit! Humans would not exist!

Humans need that core to wrap themselves around for the sake of belonging and surviving. We are social beings who seek others to communicate, belong and share.

Often the occurrence of strife is born from ignorance and perhaps the existence of a fundamental weakness in one or another. How true is it that one cannot agree with another and allow strife to survive, knowing strife divides?

Why is it so that one must persist in defiance in tongue when reality is overlooked, rather than admit to another, a wrong?

Could it be that as we have grown in thought and realities that question our origins that over the millenniums we defy our instinct and replace instinct with thought?

If that is the case, *is thought a replacement of primeval instinct?* Will thought destroy us and our family unit and allow strife to survive?

Is there a balance we need to achieve between thought and instinct to preserve our family unit?

One could argue that if thought is a replacement of our primeval instinct, we will be doomed because it is our instinct that perpetuates our existence our, survival.

So, what must cause this internal conflict between instinct and thought? Is there another element to consider?

A family unit in strife weakens the core from which it was created.

A weakened core cannot survive without the continued strength of its many parts--its house will fall--there is no longer that family unit of security which we all need and is a primeval instinct of survival.

A disagreement is good especially when, with open minds, we see the challenge of the other and embrace the argument for what it is: a thought to be discussed, not a thought to destroy our core.

We all need to heed the warning that strife brings. Strife will destroy our core security from which we hail and that it is up to us as a member of the family unit that we are obliged to keep the family unit together because in the end, our family is all we have.

The rest of what we perceive is non-superlative!

Coming of Age

It's more of an adventurous process than an end in itself!
Coming from a very vertical industry, my business relationships revolved
within that industry. Everything I did, all the marketing, communications,
point of sale processes, selling presentations, planning and trade shows
was addressed to that income stream.

Having launched a jewelry business in 1980 I developed it into a
successful international business which I then sold in two-thousand-seven.

In the process of orchestrating my business, I enjoyed the benefits and
challenges of creativity.

I enjoyed the challenges of learning, conducting research and applying
that new knowledge to my success.

I enjoyed and still do enjoy research and learning about things I do not
know and applying that knowledge to help mankind.
Fascinating!

And, learning to be creative I discovered, it is all about culture and
communications.

And, now I am discovering that communicating in the twenty-first century
is vastly different than communicating in the twentieth century.

I am learning to apply that knowledge to, become of age!

Helping Those in Need

I want to take a moment and thank AARP and the Salvation Army for the opportunity for me to recently serve those in need through the Salvation Army office in Tarpon Springs, Florida.

Although this was a temporary assignment with the Salvation Army while an employee had and recovered from an operation, I must profess that this assignment to assist those in need was the most humbling and rewarding thing I have ever experienced in my life!

Having experienced an unfortunate decline in wealth myself, I truly understand how some people may become financially dependent on strangers for financial support or needing food support even for a short time.

It has been a humbling experience and personally rewarding for me to be a small part of this chain of assistance for those in need.

Recognizing those in need would prefer not to be IN NEED, I witnessed most people to be humble and appreciative of the assistance they could get from the Salvation Army and other area supportive groups. I also witnessed that most people did not demand assistance but rather humbly accepted what assistance they could receive. I also witnessed that most if not all people accepted responsibility for their current situation and blamed no one for it.

I assisted homeless people, those in transition, local residents' temporarily needing financial assistance and, those in a job or other financial transitional period of their lives.

This humbling experience has been an eye-opener for me and has left me feeling that I have had an experience of a life time to be able to know and assist those in need!

This has been the most humbling and rewarding experience that I have ever had!

I urge all of you to find an organization serving those in need and volunteer a little of your time and experience something personal and humbling in value, in return!

Then, share your experience with the world and ask others to share and experience what you have discovered!

Time

…is always what we want more of:

- Time to be more with family

- Time for more activities

- Time to delegate activities to others

- Time to sell more products/services

- Time for more networking events

- Time to be healthy

Survival

It was a dark and stormy night, of course
Heavy rain, strong winds
Threatening destruction
A storm I could not have imagined
Threatening my existence

I search for something to combat the danger
I am alone with nothing but tangible matter,
A stranger to me
How do I fight such an impending force?
Such an intruding peril

Quickly searching
No solution apparent
My mind quickly engages the present
What choices for survival, this peril?

Without tangible evidence
I thrust myself into Super Mode
To defend my treasures to the death
Of no thought that death will occur

WHY ARE YOU HERE?

ABOUT THIS BOOK

This book is designed to offer the reader a glimpse into the mind of the author's varied challenges in sharing with mankind many diverse thoughts of interest for personal enjoyment and, to stimulate the reader to further educate oneself in the subject matter.

Various articles chosen for this book are intended for the sole purpose of educating one slightly with a topic of interest for further discussion as the reader would prefer.

These articles cover varied topics and were published over time, previous to the compilation of this, book.

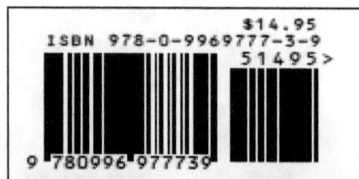

$14.95
ISBN 978-0-9969777-3-9
51495>

9 780996 977739

www.ingramcontent.com/pod-product-compliance
Lightning Source LLC
LaVergne TN
LVHW021546080426
835509LV00019B/2867